23 DUAS

FOR KIDS

ZANIB MIAN

MusLim ChiLdren's Books

For Abdullah and Abdurrahman

Published by Muslim Children's Books
Suite H, 31-33 College Road, Harrow, Middlesex HA1 1EJ

Muslim Children's Books

muslimchildrensbooks.co.uk

Published by Muslim Children's Books 2017
© Zanib Mian, 2017

Moral rights asserted.

ISBN 978-0-9955406-2-0

British Library Cataloguing in Publication Data. A catalogue record for this book is available from the British Library.

All about Duas

What are they?

Making a dua means asking Allah for things. The more you ask Allah, the more he loves you!

Everything that you need comes from Allah and He has told us to ask Him for it by making dua, and that He will respond to us. We should ask for the smallest of things, but can ask for really big things too, because Allah is the greatest - there is nothing He can't do for you or give to you. So we make dua for everything! It is us talking to Allah about our lives, like we would talk to our best friends.

When do I make them?

Don't only make dua when you're in trouble. Make dua to Allah when everything is going well too! Some duas can be made any time. Others are for particular moments.

When you've made dua, don't lose hope in Allah. He is there for us. He is forgiving, generous, kind; and he hears us. He knows us! He responds to all duas. Now, this doesn't always mean that if you ask for that new toy you saw an advert for, it will arrive straight away. That might happen, or Allah might give you something better than that and you might not even realise. He could also save you from something bad, just because you made dua.

How do I make them?

You can bring your hands up closer to your face and shoulders and look at your palms, to make dua. You can also make it without lifting your hands. You can make dua while doing anything, while riding your bike, lying in bed, cooking and lots more!

Make dua from your heart. Say it like you really mean it. This book will help you to do that, because to mean something, you have to understand it. This book will help you understand some duas from the Quran and Sunnah. They are great duas and you should learn them, but you can also make up your own duas once you get the hang of them. Remember, ask for anything and everything!

You can make duas in any language. Allah is the creator of the Universe, He knows all the languages in it!

ANXIETY AND SORROW

Everybody is sa... sometimes.

come oh, stop being lazy!

THE DUA

O Allah, I seek refuge with You from anxiety and sorrow, weakness and laziness, miserliness and cowardice, the burden of debt and from being overpowered by men.

Allahumma inni a'udhu bika minal-hammi wal-hazani wal-'ajazi wal-kasli wal-bukhli wal-jubni wa dala'id-dayni wa ghalabatir-rijal.

اللَّهُمَّ إِنِّي أَعُوذُ بِكَ مِنَ الْهَمِّ وَالْحَزَنِ، وَالْعَجْزِ، وَالْكَسَلِ، وَالْبُخْلِ، وَالْجُبْنِ، وَضَلَعِ الدَّيْنِ، وَغَلَبَةِ الرِّجَالِ

[Al- Bukhari]

what does it mean?

This means you are asking Allah for help against feeling worried about things, like how you will do in your test. Also, from feeling sad and gloomy, which is how you feel if someone upset you, or your pet died. As well as that, you're asking Allah to stop you from being weak, which isn't talking about the size of your biceps, but how strong you are inside. You're asking Him to stop you being lazy, which will help a lot when your mum tells you to tidy your room and you suddenly feel like your arms and legs are too heavy to move. As if that wasn't enough; this dua asks for Allah's help against being a coward, also known as a 'chicken' (not the small feathery animal); and against falling into a situation where you owe people money or from experiencing anything you don't want to, because other people had the power to make you.

How can I use it in my life?

Unleash the power of these words whenever you are feeling any of the emotions mentioned. Just keep saying it over and over again and it will truly help you - with Allah's will. Use it when you are too scared to go upstairs alone, after dark; or when you should be writing more for your literacy homework, but just can't be bothered; or when someone asks you for charity and you feel like holding onto the money to buy some halal jelly beans instead.

EVIL EYE

Once, I loved someone's bike so much, that they went flying over the handlebars.

The Dua

May Allah bless you.

Baarak-allaahu lakum.

بَارَكَ اللهُ لَكُمْ

[Ibn Majah]

what does it mean?

The evil eye is something harmful that happens when someone looks at something and is impressed by it. You can usually tell when someone is impressed, because the person's eyes may pop out of their sockets, or they will say words like: 'wow', 'amazing', 'cool', 'beautiful', 'I wish I had one', 'I wish I could', 'so lucky,' and so on. You can even give *yourself* the evil eye, and it can happen by accident, not only if someone is jealous of something. It won't happen every time you see something you like, but it's important to say this dua, just in case. It asks for blessings for the person who has impressed you, or for that person's belonging, which stops the evil eye in its tracks.

How can I use it in my life?

Say these words whenever you feel impressed with someone or their belongings. You could say it when your aunty buys a really cool car, or when your dad looks amazing in his new suit. You could say it when your friend gets fantastic results for their exams, or reads Quran very beautifully, or when someone makes a cake that makes you say, 'Wow!'

BEFORE EATING AND DRINKING

Ewwww warts!

Even before eating ice-cream!

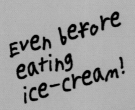

THE DUA

In the name of Allah.

Bismillah.

بِسْمِ الله

[Al- Bukhari]

what does it mean?

When you say Bismillah before eating, you are saying that you are about to put something into your mouth, so you are blessing it with the name of Allah. It's like asking Allah to watch over you eating, to make sure it's all OK and has goodness in it for you. It even makes sure that Shaytan can't share that food with you. Yes, that greedy trickster does try his very best to eat with you, if you forget to say Bismillah.

How can I use it in my life?

Say it before eating or drinking anything. Remember, if you don't, you're losing out on your food being super blessed! What's more, Shaytan will share it with you! Just imagine his slimy, wart-covered fingers trying to reach out and take a share of your scrumptious shepherd's pie! You don't want to share it with him! So, say Bismillah.

AFTER RAIN

No rain, no chocolate!

I love splashing in puddles, but my mum hates it.

THE DUA

Mutirnaa bi fadlillaahi wa rahmatih.

We have been given rain by the grace and mercy of Allah.

مُطِرْنَا بِفَضْلِ اللهِ وَرَحْمَتِهِ

[Muslim]

what does it mean?

Rain is an amazing blessing sent down by Allah. All the plants need rain, and the animals need it too, so that they can drink. If rain didn't come down, we would have no water to drink, and we wouldn't be able to grow plants for our food, or look after our animals. That's why, when it has been raining, we say this dua to show that we know it is from Allah. Allah gave us the rain because He is being kind to us and showing us mercy. If He didn't give us rain out of His mercy and grace, then the ground would look like your lips do when you haven't been drinking enough water and moisturising them! And there would be no beautiful grass growing out of it, or wheat, or cacao beans - which are where your chocolate comes from!

How can I use it in my life?

Say this dua, with a lot of appreciation, after it has rained and probably before you stomp in all the rainy, muddy puddles! You will forget to say it after the stomping, because your mum will most likely be terribly cross with you and marching you off to change your dripping wet clothes.

THANKING PEOPLE

Jazak Allah khayr for reading this.

I can't wait for my reward from Allah. I wonder what it is...

THE DUA

May Allah reward you [with] goodness.

Jazakum Allahu Khayran.

جَزَاكُمُ اللهُ خَيْراً

[Tirmidhi]

What does it mean?

This is the Islamic way of thanking someone. It is better than saying thank you, because this is a dua, which asks Allah to reward the person with goodness. When Allah rewards them with goodness, you can be sure that they have received the thanks they deserve!

How can I use it in my life?

Say it whenever you would usually say thank you, for example, when someone helps you, does something for you, or gives you something. Remember to use it the next time your adult gives you extra sprinkles on your ice-cream without you even asking!

AFTER EATING

what's the digestive system?

No heartburn for me please.

THE DUA

O Allah, bless it for us and feed us better than it.

Allahumma baarik lanaa feehi wa at'imnaa khayran minhu.

اللَّهُمَّ بَارِكْ لَنَا فِيهِ
وَأَطْعِمْنَا خَيْرًا مِنْهُ

[Ibn Majah]

what does it mean?

This dua is asking Allah to bless the food you just ate. Basically, now that all of that food has made its way inside your body, where it will be broken down and used up by your digestive system, you are asking Allah to bless it, so that it does all of that easily and only gives your body goodness. Food can otherwise be troublesome at times! It can even make you feel all hot, like your chest is on fire. You wouldn't want that (unless you are a dragon, of course)! The dua also asks Allah to give you better food, because He absolutely can!

How can I use it in my life?

Say this when you have enjoyed your scrumptious meal, wiped every grain and drop from your plate, and licked your fingers clean. You should even say it if the meal was not scrumptious, but you still smiled at your mummy or daddy and complimented the cooking.

DRINKING MILK

milk can come from goats and camels too.

I love milkshake more than anything!

THE DUA

O Allah, bless it for us and give us more of it.

Allahumma baarik lanaa feehi wa zidnaa minhu.

اللَّهُمَّ بَارِكْ لَنَا فِيهِ وَزِدْنَا مِنْهُ

[Abi Dawud]

what does it mean?

Let's be honest. Milk is awesome! It's yummy straight out of the fridge, just as it is, warmed up with a bit of honey, or blended together with ice-cream and chocolate! This dua asks Allah to bless the milk we are drinking and keep giving us more! Yes please!

How can I use it in my life?

Seriously? When drinking milk, of course!

AFRAID OF PEOPLE

help me!

Bullies can be scary.

THE DUA

O Allah, protect me from them as You wish.

Allahummak-fineehim bimaa shi'ta.

اللَّهُمَّ اكْفِنِيهِمْ بِمَا شِئْتَ

[Sahih ibn Hibban]

what does it mean?

This dua is for asking Allah to protect you from people you might be feeling scared of, for whatever reason. You're asking Allah to look after you and not let them bring any harm to you, whether it is words that may hurt you, or actual harm to your body or your things. Allah is most powerful and can protect you in so many ways – more ways than you can think of – so you ask Allah to protect you in whatever way He wishes. For example, He could turn the person's heart around, so they don't feel like harming you, or He could keep the people far away from you. Or He could make them bounce off an invisible wall, straight into a pile of stinky dinosaur waste! Yes, dinosaurs aren't around anymore, but Allah could still do that!

How can I use it in my life?

Use it at any time when you are feeling afraid of someone. This might be when you are walking down the street and there is a suspicious character. Now, in this case, you are probably just judging someone by the way they look, which isn't right, but you can use the dua just in case. It can be very handy against the school bully. You can even use it when you know that you broke your brother's favourite toy and hid it in your underwear drawer and you spot him marching towards you like a hot-headed rhino.

RELIANCE ON ALLAH

THE DUA

Allah is enough for me. There is no God but He. In Him I have put my trust. He is the Lord of the Mighty Throne.

Hasbiyal laahu laaa ilaaha illaa Huwa 'alaihi tawakkkaltu wa Huwa Rabbul 'Arshil 'Azeem.

حَسبِيَ اللَّهُ لا إِلٰهَ إِلّا هُوَ عَلَيهِ تَوَكَّلتُ وَهُوَ رَبُّ العَرشِ العَظيمِ

[Surah at-Tawbah]

what does it mean?

Just imagine relying on Allah alone. That means knowing without a doubt that Allah is there for you and will help you through anything. That means knowing that no matter how many people you ask, it is only Allah that can give you what you need, and if He wants to, then nobody in this world can stop it. Imagine feeling that way and actually seeing it happen, every time! Because when you truly rely on Allah, and not just in the way that you're pretending to yourself that you do - He will not let you down. He will be all you need, ever. Imagine you needed to find the way to do something, or find out why you are here on Earth. Imagine asking a new born baby sloth, that is helpless and not very smart, what you should do. Now think about asking the most clever, wisest man on the planet. You'd want to ask the man, right? But now, think about asking Allah, the one who has created that man and everything in the universe. The one with ALL the answers. That's who you would want to ask. And if you really ask Him, he will guide you. Lastly, imagine asking Allah, the Most Powerful, to help you, and He did. That's what this dua is: it's asking Allah to make you someone who relies on Him and trusts him. Someone who feels like Allah is enough for him.

How can I use it in my life?

Say this dua every day, but also say it at the times when you might be feeling anxious or worried about something. Or when you really want something to happen. Or when you've landed yourself in a bit of a mess and can't figure out how you'll escape it. Or when you've taken on a task, which is so big, it makes the Eiffel Tower look like a toothpick, and you don't know how you'll ever get it done.

DAILY PLEDGE

I promise...

Allah gave me so many blessings!

THE DUA

O Allah! You are my Lord! None has the right to be worshipped but You. You created me and I am Your slave, and I am faithful to my covenant and my promise as much as I can. I acknowledge before You all the blessings, and I confess to You all my sins. So, I ask You to forgive my sins, for nobody can forgive sins except You. I seek refuge with You from all the evil I have done

Allahumma anta rabbee la ilaha illa ant, Khalaq-tanee wa-ana aabduk, Wa-ana ala aah-dika wa wa'dika mas-ta-taat, Aboo-o laka bini'matika, wa-aboo-o laka bi-zan-bee, Faghfir lee fa-innahu la yagh-firu-zunooba illa ant, Aa'oozu'bika min sharri ma sanath.

اللَّهُمَّ أَنْتَ رَبِّي لاَ إِلَهَ إِلاَّ أَنْتَ، خَلَقْتَنِي وَأَنَا عَبْدُكَ، وَأَنَا عَلَى عَهْدِكَ وَوَعْدِكَ مَا اسْتَطَعْتُ، أَبُوءُ لَكَ بِنِعْمَتِكَ، وَأَبُوءُ لَكَ بِذَنْبِي، فَاغْفِرْ لِي، فَإِنَّهُ لاَ يَغْفِرُ الذُّنُوبَ إِلاَّ أَنْتَ، أَعُوذُ بِكَ مِنْ شَرِّ مَا صَنَعْتُ

[Al- Bukhari]

what does it mean?

Saying this dua means that you are standing tall and reminding yourself that Allah is your Lord and that you believe that nobody else or nothing else has the right to be worshipped – just Him. We love Allah so much that we want to shout this from the roof-tops every day, but because that wouldn't be so practical, we can say this dua from the depths of our hearts instead. The dua says that you believe that He made you and you want to do all the things He wants you to do, for Him. You are at His service. Yes sir! You know that He has told us through the Quran and Sunnah how to live our lives, and you promise to live yours that way. You ask Him to help you against the bad things you have done. You tell Allah that you know how many amazing favours He has done for you, like giving you blessings. So you ask for his forgiveness, because nobody can forgive sins except Him.

How can I use it in my life?

If you have said this dua on the day or the night that you die, you will go to heaven. So say it every morning and every evening. It helps you remember who is in charge of this whole world, whose rules you should be following, who gives you everything that you have, and who can forgive you if you slip up.

SAFETY

The Universe is big!

Nothing can harm me now!

THE DUA

In the name of Allah with whose name nothing is harmed on Earth nor in the heavens and He is The All-Seeing, The All-Knowing.

Bismil-lahil-lazee la-yadurru ma'aas-mihi shay-un fil-ardi wala fis-sama-i wahuwas-samee'ul-aa'leem.

بِسْمِ اللَّهِ الَّذِي لاَ يَضُرُّ مَعَ اسْمِهِ شَيْءٌ فِي الأَرْضِ وَلاَ فِي السَّمَاءِ وَهُوَ السَّمِيعُ الْعَلِيمُ

[Abi Dawud]

what does it mean?

You know this Earth was made by Allah. Well so were all the other planets, like Mars, Mercury, and Venus. He even made the Sun, the Moon and all the other solar systems and galaxies in the whole universe! He made them and He controls everything that happens in them. When we say this dua, we are saying that with Allah's name, nothing can be harmed on Earth or even in space! We are saying that He sees everything and He knows everything that is going on, so He sure can protect it!

How can I use it in my life?

Say this dua every day, three times, and nothing will harm you.
How super-awesome is that?!

GLORIFYING ALLAH

Allah is the greatest!

I give my mum big hugs!

THE DUA

All Glory is to Allah and all Praise to Him, Glorified is Allah, the Great.

Subhanallahi wa bi-hamdihi, Subhanallahil-azim.

سُبْحَانَ اللهِ وَبِحَمْدِهِ،

سُبْحَانَ اللهِ الْعَظِيم

[Al- Bukhari]

what does it mean?

You know how you're always asking your mum for things: food, clean clothes, help with homework, or a bedtime story? But you don't only talk to her or about her when you want something. Sometimes you just go up to her and give her a hug, or tell her you love her and that she's the best mummy in the world. Well this dua is like that. It's when you're not asking Allah for something, but you're just telling Him how great He is and how glad you are for all the things He does for you all the time! You're telling Allah that He is super, magnificent, the most impressive, the greatest, and most brilliant – He is glorious and the one to be thanked for everything!

How can I use it in my life?

Say this dua all the time - whenever you want. Say it when you are looking at the clouds, mountains, trees or the sea and thinking: *wow, Allah is so glorious – all this is His, and He made it!* Say it when you're not even looking at anything, but just thinking about Allah and how much you love Him. And guess what? Allah loves that you say these words so much, that He forgives your sins and gives you more rewards than you'd be able to count.

ALLAH'S LOVE

Allah loves you too.

see?! Allah loves me!

THE DUA

O Allah! I ask You for Your love and the love of those who love You, and for the love of actions which will bring me closer to Your love.

Allahumma inni as aluka hubbaka, wa hubba man yuhibbuka, wa hubba 'amalin yuqarribuni ila hubbika.

اللَّهُمَّ اِنِّن أَسْئَلُكَ حُبَّكَ

وحُبَّ مَنْ يُّحِبُّكَ

وحُبَّ عَمَلٍ يُّقَرِّبُ اِلى حُبِّكَ

[Al- Bukhari]

what does it mean?

Allah already loves you, even without you asking. Allah actually loves you more than your own mother does! Not just a little bit more, but seventy times more! That means that if your mum's love for you was the size of a cat, Allah's love for you is at least the size of a whopping Tyranusaurus rex! Now just imagine, Allah, who has power and control over all things, loves you that much more than your own mum! And what's more, this dua asks Him for more of His love. It makes sure that love is looked after, like a flower is with sunlight and water. It also asks for the love of those that love Allah, which will make the best company for you and help you get to Jannah, and asks to be able to do things which will make Allah love you even more!

How can I use it in my life?

Use this dua whenever you are feeling a love for Allah, and even when it has been a while since you last felt your heart inflate like a helium balloon and carry you over the trees with your love for Allah.

Use it as often as you can. You'll see how good it feels!

AFTER BEING HORRIBLE

make up for it!

Once, I told my sister that I hate her.

The Dua

O Allah, whomever of the believers I have abused, make that a means of closeness to You on the Day of Resurrection.

Allahuma fa ayyumaa mu'minin sababtuhu faj'al thaalika lahu qurbatan ilaika yawmal-qiyaamati.

اللَّهُمَّ فَأَيُّمَا مُؤْمِنٍ سَبَبْتُهُ

فَاجْعَلْ ذَلِكَ لَهُ قُرْبَةً إِلَيْكَ

يَوْمَ الْقِيَامَةِ

[Al- Bukhari]

what does it mean?

We can all get a bit hot under the collar sometimes, and forget how to get rid of Shaytan, before we let out some horrid words towards another person. When this happens, we also tend to feel guilty for it later, and wish we could take the words back. But we can't. What we can do, is make this dua for that person. This is asking Allah to take away some of the person's bad deeds and show the person His mercy, because of the hurtful things you might have said to them, like: "Get out of my room, you stinky sausage breath!" or, "You look so ugly with that spot."

How can I use it in my life?

Say this dua at that time when you start feeling that creeping guilt about having hurt someone - when you keep stealing glances at them to see if they're OK - or when you want to phone them but are too scared that they won't want to talk to you anymore. You should say it right after you have said something terrible to someone, but you probably won't realise you need to say it until you calm down. Things will be better if you use this dua and apologise.

VEHICLES

I love horse riding!

I wish I was an astronaut.

THE DUA

All praise is for Allah. Glory be to Him, who has subjected this unto our service. We could never have done it by ourselves. And to our Lord shall we surely return.

Al-hamdu lillaahi, subhaana alladhi sakhkhara lana hadha wa maa kunna lahu muqrineen, wa inna ila rabbinaa lamunqalibun.

الْحَمْدُ لِلَّهِ، سُبْحَانَ الَّذِي سَخَّرَ لَنَا هَذَا وَمَا كُنَّا لَهُ مُقْرِنِينَ، وَإِنَّا إِلَى رَبِّنَا لَمُنْقَلِبُونَ

[Surah al-Zukhruf]

what does it mean?

This dua means that we are thanking Allah and saying how great He is, for giving us the car or aeroplane or even rocket, tractor, monster truck, that we are travelling in or the animal that we are riding on and we are showing that we know that it's because of Allah that we are able to control our ride. It's because of Him that it doesn't go crazy and start crashing into everything in sight! We could not control it without Allah's will. You're saying that Allah is completely perfect and one day we will go back to Him. Yay!

How can I use it in my life?

Say this dua whenever you get into a vehicle or onto an animal, which is going to take you from A to B. So, whenever you're on the bus, train, or in a car. Also when you finally accomplish your dream of becoming an astronaut, or when you finally get to ride a pony, you can say it to keep you safe.

SICKNESS

yucky medicine!

pass me a tissue please.

THE DUA

No harm, may it be a purification for you, if Allah wills.

La ba'sa, tahuurun in shaa Allah.

لَا بَأْسَ، طَهُورٌ إِنْ شَاءَ اللهُ

[Al- Bukhari]

what does it mean?

This dua is a huge comfort for someone who is ill, and undoubtedly feeling sorry for themselves because their arms and legs feel like jelly and perhaps there is a tiny tap up their nose, which has been turned on at full force. The dua is assuring the sick person that it's ok. It's all fine, because sins are being taken away from them because of how they are feeling.

How can I use it in my life?

This dua is for other people, so say it to your friends and family when they are sick. You can gather lots of good rewards from Allah for yourself when you go and visit someone, just because they are unwell, and say this dua to them.

THIS WORLD, NEXT WORLD

Goodness me.

I say this dua all the time!

THE DUA

My Lord, give us good in this world, and also good in the next world, and deliver us from the torment of hell fire.

Rabbana aatina fid-dunya hasanatan wa fil 'akhirati hasana-tan waqina 'adhaban-nar.

﴿رَبَّنا آتِنا فِي الدُّنيا حَسَنَةً وَفِي الآخِرَةِ حَسَنَةً وَقِنا عَذابَ النّارِ﴾

[Surah al-Baqarah]

what does it mean?

This dua is very complete, because we aren't only asking Allah for all the things that we want and need in this world, we are also asking Him for goodness in the next life, and to save us from the fire (in hell). And He surely will, because He loves us! So it's all sorted! Goodness in this life and goodness in the next life too, In sha Allah! But we have to do our bit – so keep being the best you!

How can I use it in my life?

This was the dua that the Prophet (salallahu alayhi wasallam) used to say the most! So let's make it the one we say the most too!

KNOWLEDGE

my grandma needs her glasses to read.

THE DUA

O' my lord, increase me in knowledge.

Rabbi zidni 'ilma.

﴿ رَبِّ زِدْنِي عِلْمًا ﴾

[Surah Taha]

what does it mean?

Knowing things is amazing! How something works, how to do something, how to build something, how to speak in other languages, and the most beautiful of all – knowing Allah! Knowing what He told us about how to live our lives and how to treat others. Knowing the words of the Quran and what they mean. Knowing the stories of the prophets, and the hadith and the Seerah of Prophet Muhammad (sallAllahu alayhi wa sallam). Knowing makes you feel good, and can get you out of a pickle too! This dua asks Allah to make what you know, much much more, so that you can learn new things.

How can I use it in my life?

Now, obviously, this is a great one to use when you are studying or about to take an exam, but knowledge is one of the greatest things you could ask for in this world, so ask for it a lot! You super genius, you!

UNDERSTANDING OF DEEN

I want to get it right.

seriously, read the instructions!

THE DUA

O Allah, grant me understanding of the deen.

Allahmuma Faqqihnee Fid-deen.

اللَّهُمَّ فَقِّهْنِي فِي الدِّينِ

[Al- Bukhari]

what does it mean?

Through this dua we ask Allah to help us to really and truly understand the deen, which is our religion and the way we live our lives. What could be more important than that?! If people don't know what they are doing, or how to do it, they are bound to end up in a heap of mess. For example, if you saw your friend trying to turn a phone on by dipping it in a bowl of soup, you'd think they were totally nuts. Surely, your friend should learn how to use the phone, to get a good understanding of it! That way the phone might actually turn on and allow your friend to do lots of fabulous things with it. We have to ask Allah to help us understand the deen, so we know exactly what kind of things Allah likes us to do, what He doesn't like us to do; and how we should treat others, the earth, our wealth and lots more!

How can I use it in my life?

Make this dua all the time, but especially when you find that you don't understand something about the deen. Sometimes different people understand the deen in different ways – ask Allah to guide you to understand it the way He meant.

PAIN & ILLNESS

Once, I dropped a mango oh my foot. It hurt.

I know the story of prophet Ayub.

THE DUA

O my Lord, great harm has afflicted me and You are the Most Merciful of the merciful!

Rabbi inni massani-yadh-urru wa 'anta arhamur-Raahimeen.

﴿رَبِّ إِنِّي مَسَّنِيَ الضُّرُّ وَأَنتَ أَرْحَمُ الرّاحِمِينَ﴾

[Surah al-Anbiya]

what does it mean?

This is the dua of Prophet Ayub (alayhi salaam). It's really wonderful, because you are reaching out to Allah, the only one who can heal you, and the one who cares and listens to your complaints. You're telling Allah that you are sick, or in pain, and He is the most merciful one. You're asking for Him to have mercy on you and take away the pain.

How can I use it in my life?

Say this dua if you happen to get hurt by flying over the handlebars of your bike, when you thought you could build a ramp in your garden and do super-cool bike stunts. You might have to say it if you step on a tiny piece of lego on your carpet (see the benefit of tidying up now?).You can say it when you have a sore throat, chicken pox, or any kind of illness or pain.

CHARACTER

If you smile, you will always look nice.

I'm shiny from the inside.

THE DUA

O Allah, as you have perfected my physical form, so too perfect my character.

Allahumma kama ahsanta khalqi fa ahsin khuluqi.

اللَّهُمَّ كَمَا أَحْسَنْتَ خَلْقِي فَأَحْسِنْ خُلُقِي

[Abi Dawud]

what does it mean?

This dua helps us remember that a person's beauty comes from more than just the colour of their eyes, or the shape of their nose, or how high their cheekbones are. It comes from how kind they are, how patient they are, how much they love Allah and other characteristics of behaviour. The dua reminds us that it's more important to have perfect character than a perfect physical appearance and asks Allah to help us achieve that. It also shows gratitude to Allah for giving us the physical features; like eyes, nose, arms and legs, that He chose for us.

How can I use it in my life?

Say this dua if you look in the mirror, or think about the way you look. You can even say it if someone compliments the way you look by saying how pretty or handsome you are!

GRATITUDE

This means being thankful.

Alhamdulillah, I can see!

Alhamdulilah

THE DUA

My Lord, enable me to be thankful for the blessing You have bestowed on me and on my parents, and keep me acting rightly, pleasing You, and admit me, by Your mercy, among Your righteous servants.

Rabbi awzi'nee an ashkura ni'mataka allatee an'amta 'alayya wa 'ala walidayya waan a'mala salihan tardahu wa adkhilnee birahmatika fee 'ibadikaassaliheen.

﴿رَبِّ أَوْزِعْنِي أَنْ أَشْكُرَ نِعْمَتَكَ الَّتِي أَنْعَمْتَ عَلَيَّ وَعَلَى وَالِدَيَّ وَأَنْ أَعْمَلَ صَالِحًا تَرْضَاهُ وَأَدْخِلْنِي بِرَحْمَتِكَ فِي عِبَادِكَ الصَّالِحِينَ﴾

[Surah an-Naml]

what does it mean?

Sometimes, we can completely forget just how blessed we are. We are so used to having those blessings that we don't notice them anymore. For example, when was the last time you woke up and said: "Ah! Alhamdulillah, my nose is still there. Yep, I can definitely still detect the smelly socks on my floor and the waffles cooking downstairs." Everything we have is a blessing that we should feel really thankful for - from our joints and our senses, to our homes and family and much, much more. This wonderful dua from the Quran asks Allah to help us to remember all the blessings He has given us and our parents and to be thankful for them. It also asks Allah to make sure we only do things which are right. Things that please Him. And we ask Him, by His mercy, to make us amongst the best and excellent of those who worship him.

How can I use it in my life?

Say this dua all the time so that you don't forget that there are many people in this world who would look at you and say: "So lucky!"
This is because you have been given many blessings by Allah. What's great is, that the more thankful you are for everything you have, the more Allah gives you!

FOR THE PROPHET

I hope I can be like him.

The Prophet (saw) was very patient.

THE DUA

Oh Allah! Send your mercy upon (Holy Prophet) Muhammad and upon the family of (Holy Prophet) Muhammad as You sent blessings upon Ibraheem and upon the family of Ibraheem; indeed, You are praiseworthy and glorious. And send your blessings upon (Holy Prophet) Muhammad and the family of (Holy Prophet) Muhammad as You blessed Ibraheem and the family of Ibraheem; indeed, You are praise worthy and glorious.

Allahumma salli ala Muhammadin wa 'ala aali Muhammadin kama sallayta 'ala Ibrahima wa 'ala aali Ibrahima innaka hamidun majeed. Wa baarik 'ala Muhammadin wa 'ala aali sayyidina Muhammadin kama baarakta 'ala Ibrahima wa 'ala aali sayyidina Ibrahima innaka hamidun majeed.

اللَّهُمَّ صَلِّ عَلَى مُحَمَّدٍ، وَعَلَى آلِ مُحَمَّدٍ، كَمَا صَلَّيْتَ عَلَى إِبْرَاهِيمَ، وَعَلَى آلِ إِبْرَاهِيمَ، إِنَّكَ حَمِيدٌ مَجِيدٌ، وَبَارِكْ عَلَى مُحَمَّدٍ، وَعَلَى آلِ مُحَمَّدٍ، كَمَا بَارَكْتَ عَلَى إِبْرَاهِيمَ، وَعَلَى آلِ إِبْرَاهِيمَ، إِنَّكَ حَمِيدٌ مَجِيدٌ

[Al- Bukhari]

what does it mean?

This dua is specially for our beloved Prophet (salallahu alayhi wasallam). It asks Allah to send His mercy and blessings on him and his family, just like Allah had sent mercy and blessings on the Prophet Ibrahim's (alayhi salaam) family. Saying this dua shows our love for our Prophet (salallahu alayhi wasallam), it shows that we really appreciate everything he did for us as Allah's messenger. He struggled a lot and had to face many difficult situations, all so that we could find out that Allah is one, and how to worship Him.

How can I use it in my life?

Say this dua as often as possible. There are so many blessings and benefits for you, just for reciting it, that your eyes would pop out of your head if you could see them!

Did you know, that there are some times and some places when it's even better to make dua?! Here are some examples:

Laylat al-Qadar.

During the night, before dawn.

After salah.

Between the adhaan and the iqaamah.

When rain falls.

When drinking zamzam water.

When prostrating.

When hearing the crowing of a rooster.

Du'aa' for somebody who is sick.

Dua for parents.

write your own dua

....

....

....

....

....

....

....

....

....

Other fantastic titles by Zanib Mian

www.muslimchildrensbooks.co.uk

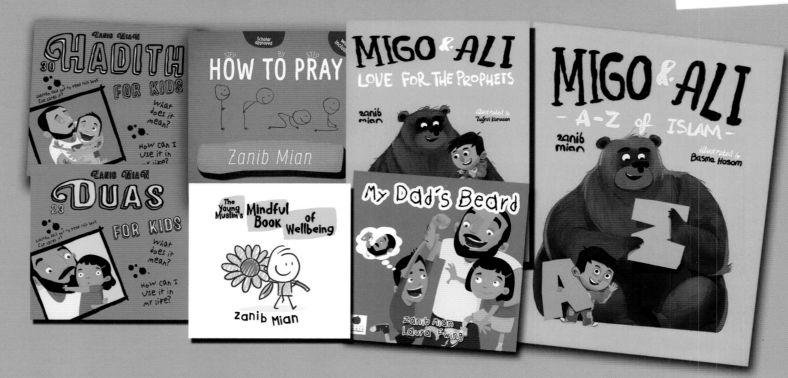

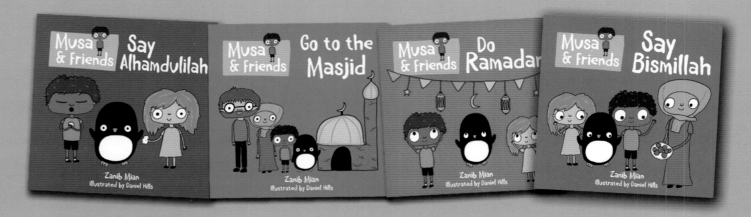